To Dan

Mar 2, '07

Tell It Like It Is

Ed Reitz

II Tim. 1:7

Ed Reitz

Tell It Like It Is

Ed Reitz

PUBLISHED BY:
BRENTWOOD CHRISTIAN PRESS
4000 BEALLWOOD AVENUE
COLUMBUS, GEORGIA 31904

This book is affectionately
dedicated to my wife, Jene Sue, who has
lent great support and encouragement
in the writing of this book
and believes wholeheartedly
in the premises found in these pages.

Contents

Introduction

Shortly after moving to Palm Desert, California, I discovered that I lived close to a preserve for the fringe-toed lizard. For reasons that were difficult for me to understand, 1000 acres had been set aside for the preservation of this small creature that I had never seen or even heard about. In addition, it was desert land and high winds frequently blew over the preserve and covered our patios, swimming pools and everything else we owned with fine particles of sand—to say nothing of contaminating the air we breathe.

Then there is a friend of mine, Ron Yanke, who owned three thriving saw mills in central California. He was forced to shut down two of them, lay off hundreds of employees, all because of a bird called the Spotted Owl. One million acres of forest land was designated as the private domain of this feathered creature, and lumber could no longer be profitably transported to his mills

How did we get here? When did a lizard become more important than the air we breathe or the lifestyle we lead? When did the preservation of a little known winged creature become more critical than the livelihood of lumberjacks and workers who needed to care for their families?

The answer to those questions is what we are wrestling over in this book. Our purpose is to look back into the recent history of the United States and much of the rest of the world and seek to analyze the most poignant events that brought about the changes.

In addition to these flagrant changes in our attitude toward the importance of living things, our world has undergone many changes that leave many of us aghast, who remember what life was like just 50 or 60 years ago.

Now the points of view that will be taken here are not the views of some narrow minded, ostentatious conservative with his head in the sand. Rather, in spite of 50 or so years of indoctrination to the contrary, many Americans and many citizens in the world at large will agree with the tenets set forth in this book.

I make no apology for any of the arguments that are set forth in this treatise. The recognition of their truth could change the future of nations, and at least it is my hope and prayer that it will awaken the minds of some who have never taken the opportunity to explore their premises.

Some of the views expressed may for a few put me the camp of Don Feder, columnist for the Boston Herald, who was described by William Jefferson Clinton, while president of the United States, as a "fanatic" spreading a message of "hate and fear." * But putting that risk aside, let me say that I am approaching my world with love, not hate and since "perfect love drives out fear" ** there seems to be no excuse for a fearful attitude.

The subjects discussed in this treatise will be considered controversial. I am only asking that the reader come with an open mind and heart and consider, before making any final judgment, whether the facts presented are truthful.

While discussing the premises of the evolutionist, I am recognizing that the indoctrination into this theory is long standing. I therefore have no right or reason to be hateful toward his view. And when speaking of the homosexual lifestyle I am neither homophobic, meaning that I fear homosexuals, nor do I hate them. On the contrary, I genuinely love them.

While working at the Betty Ford Center as a substitute for the Pastoral Care Counselor, my supervisor, who happened to be a Roman Catholic nun, couldn't understand how I could do well in counseling homosexuals knowing my attitude toward homosexuality. The answer was not puzzling. I got along very well with them, loving the person, not the lifestyle he was in.

So judge for yourself, as we grapple with the radical changes that have occurred in the last 50 or 60 years in America and in our world. Our beginning point will be the theory of evolution and the dramatic effect it has had on our world.

---

* Feder, Don, *Who's Afraid of the Religious Right.* Ottowa, Illinois: Jameson Books, 1996, pg. 3.
** I John 4:18 (NIV)

Chapter One

EVOLUTION OR CREATION?

Since the question of whether we descended from lower forms of life has drastically reshaped the thinking of most all of the civilized world, we will begin our discussion here.

Although Charles Darwin was not the first to propose the theory of the evolutionary process that resulted in man, his writings, "The Origin of Species" and "The Descent of Man" were the ones that caused the spiral of thinking that was destined to encircle the globe. "The Origin of Species" appeared on November 24, 1859 with 1,250 copies in the first edition, all of which were sold on the day of publication.

Charles Darwin was the son of a highly successful physician, who sent him to Edinburgh to study medicine. However he showed more interest in animals, tidal pools and oysters than he did in medicine. His father's next attempt was to send him to Cambridge to study to be a minister of the Gospel, but again his interests were diverted and he became an ardent entomologist.

Anyone who has done any serious reading in these two treatises mentioned above, knows that to Darwin his writings were a theory, not science as they are purported to be today. For example, the title of his sixth chapter in "The Origin of Species" is "Difficulties of the Theory." [1] and in his summary of Chapter VIII, he refers to "my theory" and "the theory of natural selection." [2]

Today this theory of evolution is taught across America and around the world as science. The word "science" comes from its basic root which means "to know." But after decades of geological, biological and fossil findings the quest is still to find enough data to take it out of the realm of speculation and theory and place it in the ranks of knowledge.

And that will never happen, because it is still just that—a theory and not a set of identifiable facts that could be called science.

Darwin pointed out four difficulties of his theory in Chapter VI, and those difficulties exist to this day. (1) "...why, if species have descended from other species by fine gradations, do we not everywhere see innumerable transitional forms? Why is not all nature in confusion, instead of the species being, as we see them, well defined? (2) "...Can we believe that natural selection could produce, on the one hand, an organ of trifling importance, such as the tail of a giraffe, which serves as a fly-flapper, and, on the other hand, an organ so wonderful as the eye?" (3) "Can instincts be acquired and modified through natural selection? (4) "...how can we account for species, when crossed, being sterile and producing sterile offspring, whereas, when varieties are crossed, their fertility is unimpaired?" [3]

Darwin wrestled with some possible answers to these questions to fit his theory, but neither his answers nor almost 150 years of research have brought a satisfactory answer.

Another difficulty with the theory is that all of nature has what we would call "design." How can there be design without a designer? All of the elements in nature have very specific, identifiable design. This question has come to clear focus recently in the State of Ohio, where the Ohio Board of Education called a public meeting where the pros and cons of the concept of intelligent design were discussed. About 1,500 people showed up for the discussion. The concept has been called ID, and the Massachusetts Institute of Technology Press issued an 805 page anthology entitled "Intelligent Design Creationism and Its Critics."

What is not universally known is that there are hundreds of scientists who accept the biblical view of creation, some who have struggled long and hard before coming to the conclusion that there is no better answer than that what we have in nature comes from the hand of the Creator. There are over 600 scientists who are members of the Institute for Creation Research, all of whom would attest to the biblical account of creation. Recently, Dr. John F. Ashton brought together the writings of 50 scientists who have chosen to believe in creation "in six days," and that is the title to the book. [4]

Unfortunately Darwinism has gained a monopoly in school systems around the world. Here in the United States, the concept of intelligent design, "gaps" in the fossil record and the pervasive pattern of sudden appearance of new life forms followed by long periods of no change are causing a slight dent in the armor of the devout Darwinians. But text books and most publications still proclaim evolution as fact and science, not theory, as it should rightfully be called.

But the real tragedy is what this virus of evolution has caused. Since it is accepted that man ascended from lower forms of animal life, rather than being "created in the image of God," then he has no authority higher than himself to answer to. All moral values are relative, since there is no God to whom one must answer. Furthermore there is no hope of anything beyond this life. We came from animals, we die like animals.

And if the foundation is flawed, whatever one builds upon it will be flawed as well. So it is in the world today, and we will trace some of the ramifications of building human life and values around this flawed foundation. But before we do so let's look at the tenets of these two dramatically different concepts—evolution and creation.

The Tenets of the Evolutionist

The Evolutionist begins with the "scientific fact" that man has indeed evolved from lower forms of life. Because of varying discoveries in geological strata and fossil records, plus individual attitudes of scientists, not all will be in agreement as to the evolutionary process. But all will agree that man owes his existence to evolution.

The concept of "natural selection" or "survival of the fittest" as taken from Darwin's theory remains a strategic focus of the continuing studies.

Reliance on radio active testing to determine the age of fossils, objects or the earth's strata is necessary to account for the drastic changes in all forms of life as we experience them today.

All matter and all living things are presumed to have come from some pre-existing state and the process is relegated to chance or accident, with the exception of some recent thinking regarding the necessity of intelligent design or ID.

The Tenets of the Creationist

The Creationist begins with observing all forms of life and matter and believing that they came into existence as the result of a divine being called Creator. All geological, biological and other scientific studies are considered observations to better understand the nature of what the Creator has put on this planet and in the vast universes and galaxies above and around us on planet earth.

Most creationists and most scientists who are creationists accept the biblical record of creation. This record is found throughout the entire Bible, not merely in a few chapters in Genesis. In Deuteronomy the writer speaks about "…the day God created man on the earth."[5] The Psalmists make several references to the God of Creation. The prophet Isaiah states "… he who fashioned and made the earth, he founded it; he did not create it to be empty, but formed it to be inhabited—he says 'I am the Lord, and there is no other'."[6] The prophet Malachi writes "Have we not all one Father? Did not one God create us?"[7] And then in the New Testament record in the Gospel of John, and in two of the letters of the Apostle Paul, the statement is made that Jesus Christ, the Son of God, also participated in creation.[8,9,10]

Let's look more closely at these opposing views—first, evolution. The first and most obvious flaw in the theory is one we have already touched upon. Even our own basic concept of logic will tell us that anything with design must of necessity have a designer. Years ago a college course in logic was taught and students were expected to use their reasoning powers to come to logical conclusions. It is not logical to presume that an absolutely gorgeous Bird of Paradise flower somehow knew to design itself, or that a camel knew to develop a retaining system for water so that it could survive on long journeys through the desert sands. The same could be said for an infinite number of living things.

The presupposition that geologic formations required a long period of time must come into question when we consider the eruption of Mount St. Helens. Here the cataclysmic forces produced geologic effects that resembled other earth strata, that previously were considered to have taken millions of years to develop. And earth dating methods apply assumptions about how things occurred in the past. Dr. Jeremy I. Walter, head of the Engineering Analysis and Design Department at Pennsylvania State University, points out that methods used for "...estimating the age of the earth or of the universe apply assumptions about processes and rates that extend into the distant past. Regardless of how apparently compelling such dating methods may appear to be, the fact remains that they are built on assumptions that must be critically questioned and evaluated."[11]

Then there are the four problems in the theory that Darwin brought up in his book, "The Origin of Species," which we mentioned previously. The first one is why there are not innumerable transitional forms everywhere, and why do we see only species that are well defined? Neither Darwin nor anyone else studying this issue have been able to come up with a satisfactory explanation.

The second problem addressed the issue of how "natural selection" could produce both trifling organs like the tail of a giraffe, which appears to serve as a fly-flapper, and yet produce so refined an organ as the eye. To further elongate this problem, many species require highly refined organs and could not conceivably survive with an organ in transition.

The third problem addressed was that of instincts being acquired or modified through "natural selection." Once again, neither Darwin, now any succeeding scientist has come up with a logical answer.

The fourth problem Darwin faced was the fact that when different species are crossed the offspring is sterile, whereas when varieties of the same species are crossed fertility is not impaired. Evolutionary theory does not have an answer that meets the perimeters of logic.

Today's evolutionists have gone far beyond Darwinian theory. They have, for the most part, taken the position that there is no Creator behind all of this, which Darwin did not do. They have accepted the theory as "fact" and "science" and find no room for other possibilities, in spite of the fact that the theory is essentially flawed.

Then there is the matter of water on planet earth. How did our oceans originate? There is no evidence that water exists on any other planet within our universe, and yet water is here in abundance and absolutely necessary for the preservation of life.

Furthermore there is balance on our planet. It is well known that changes in our atmosphere, temperature or a variety of conditions could make this planet uninhabitable. How could evolutionary process over billions of years bring about this great miracle of balance?

The biblical account of "...plants bearing seed according to their kinds and trees bearing fruit with seed in it according to their kinds"[12] is the same condition we experience today. Variations through very sophisticated horticulture are well known, but the basic principle of seed producing its own kind remains. We have no reason to believe it was ever any different.

A great deal more "faith" is required to believe in the evolutionary process than to believe the biblical account of creation. To believe in an evolutionary process within a species due to climate, geographical and other changes are well within the boundaries of understanding, but not the crossovers that ultimately produced man.

In contrast, the creationist believes that man came into being by the will and purpose of a Creator. This Creator designed man after his own image. Man was given dominion over the earth and over the animals of the earth. He disobeyed God soon after his arrival but the God of Creation has been seeking his company and favor ever since. According to the writings of the Apostle Paul

"...what may be known about God is plain to them, because God has made it plain to them. For since the creation of the world God's invisible qualities—his eternal power and divine nature—have been clearly seen, being understood from what has been made, so that men are without excuse."[13]

Why then has mankind gone down the steep descent away from the knowledge of God in creation, especially since there is so little empirical evidence to back up this theory of evolution? There can be little doubt that the underlying reason is that in accepting the theory of evolution as fact, mankind is no longer required to adhere to any laws outside of himself. Since we have moved several steps beyond Darwin's theory, making it fact, and eliminating any Creator then we are free to design our own value system, our own understanding of morality and literally have made ourselves "God." It sounds reminiscent of the story of man's first temptation, "...and you will be like God..."[14]

One thing is sure. There has been a distinct evolutionary process in what mankind has done with Darwin's theory. Most every textbook in America, science journals, newspapers and nearly all forms of media reach out for the next fossil finding and herald it as though we are coming closer and closer to understanding our origin.

But the strange fact remains. When surveys are done across America an overwhelming majority of our people profess to believe in God, and religious observance continues at a rather high level.

Nevertheless if we accept evolution as it is now being taught around the world, that there is no god, but man himself, we have no one to believe in or to worship.

Again there is a biblical answer. The Apostle Paul proclaims that the Creator has done some writing on men's hearts. "...They show that the requirements of the law are written on their hearts, their consciences also bearing witness..."[15] And we are shown the reason for our condition—"...although they knew God, they neither glorified him as God nor gave thanks to him, but their thinking became futile and their foolish hearts were darkened."[16]

Well, that's not a very pretty picture. And although what Paul told the Roman Church was a universal condition, we have seen some steep descent in our nation and in our world that has been rather dramatic over the last 50 or 60 years.

In succeeding chapters we will trace that descent away from the knowledge of the Creator and the laws of the Creator.

Endnotes

1.   Darwin, Charles. *Origin of Species.* Chicago, Illinois: Great Books of the Western World, Encyclopedia Britannica, Inc.,1952, page 80.

2.   Darwin, Charles. *Origin of Species.* Chicago, Illinois: Great Books, Encyclopedia Britannica, Inc., 1952, page 134-135.

3.   Darwin, Charles. *Origin of Species.* Chicago, Illinois: Great Books, Encyclopedia Britannica, Inc., 1952, page 80.

4.   Ashton, John. *In Six Days.* Green Forest, Arkansas: Master Books, 2001.

5.   Deuteronomy 4:32 (NIV)

6.   Isaiah 45:18 (NIV)

7.   Malachi 2:10 (NIV)

8, 9, 10. John 1:3, Ephesians 3:9, Colossians 1:16 (NIV)

11. Ashton, John. *In Six Days,* Green Forest, Arkansas: Master Books, 2001, page 13.

12. Genesis 1:12 (NIV)

13. Romans 1:19-20 (NIV)

14. Genesis 3:4 (NIV)

15. Romans 2:15 (NIV)

16. Romans 1:21 (NIV)

Chapter Two

THE SEXUAL REVOLUTION

The sexual revolution followed quite naturally the teaching of the seriously flawed theory of evolution. It appeared like a newfound freedom. And the more we exercised our sexual freedom, the more devotedly we taught evolution, until the concept of creation was relegated to the narrow minded, primitive religionist and not permitted in the textbooks of our nation, and other nations around the world.

Of course what has occurred in the sexual revolution is not entirely new to mankind. Throughout man's history, deviation from the laws of God in sexual behavior has been obvious, with some periods of history more flagrant than others. But in Western civilization it is very apparent that sexual behavior and attitudes toward it have changed rapidly over the last few decades.

In this chapter we will discuss the varied facets the sexual revolution has had, their effect on the individual, the society and the ultimate effect on the destiny of mankind.

Promiscuity

When a young bride came down the aisle, all dressed in white, on the arm of her father, it was originally supposed to mean that she was coming as a virgin. She was being presented to the church, and the church was presenting her to her virgin husband. And, believe it or not, there are still virgin brides coming to the altar of marriage to marry virgin husbands. And there are thousands of young people who have taken vows of abstinence from sexual intercourse until after marriage.

In most of our modern society, of course, that is not the case. Very early on our teenagers are made to feel that sexual intercourse is accepted and expected. Most sex education courses only set the stage for experimentation and those who do not engage in sex are considered odd.

To add to this picture, the television and movie industry consider it necessary to portray vivid sexual scenes in order to captivate the interests of their audiences. Pre-marital or adulterous sexual relationships are the rule of the day.

The obvious follows. Babies are conceived due to inadequate birth control measures, lack of knowledge or a variety of reasons. Now what shall we do about unwanted pregnancies? Some of the solutions set forth include providing condoms in the school clinics, more instruction in the sex education classes and finally recommending abortion, with or without parental knowledge or approval.

The long term effect on marriage, family and our society becomes fairly plain. Again the results are not new to any society, but the magnitude of the problem is new. Couple after couple are now content to live together without the benefit of matrimony. Children are born in homes where their parents have different last names. Often the unions are not stable, resulting in single parent families.

Abortion

It followed naturally that the sexual revolution produced many unwanted pregnancies. In 1972 the Supreme Court of the United States, in Rowe versus Wade, made the unprecedented decision that abortion was an acceptable answer. From that day to today, millions of unborn babies have suffered the fate of an untimely death.

To make it all sound more palatable, we have adopted a new vocabulary to describe what is taking place. We describe some of our young people as "sexually active," making sure there are no moral overtones. We call abortion "terminating an unwanted pregnancy."

And then we have the phrase "the woman's right to choose." But who is this woman to whom we are giving the power of life and death? Is she a happily married woman? No, usually a happily married woman is eager to have a baby. The woman we are giving the right to choose is usually a teenager or a young woman who has been caught up in our amoral society with no one giving guidelines of what is right and what is wrong.

Abortion has become a highly debated, political issue. From the "right to choose" advocates we hear that it is the woman's constitutional right to allow her unborn baby to be killed. In the United Stated abortion has been legal only 30 years. Before Rowe versus Wade couples wanting to adopt had a much easier time. Now it is difficult to locate a pregnant woman who is willing to bring the baby to term for an adopting couple.

Abortion is being used as an alternate method of birth control. The fact that a human life has begun is set aside. Often abortion is ending the beating of a human heart and in partial birth abortion a life is being ended that potentially has the capacity to survive outside the womb. This is all difficult for those of us who were raised to respect human life. And transgression at this level only opens the door to further disrespect for the lives of the elderly, mentally ill or retarded or others who have "less value" or the ability to contribute to society.

The framers of the Constitution of the United States had no idea that a Supreme Court would ever assert their power in proclaiming that abortion was some kind of "right." In fact Article III states that the judges of the Supreme Court "shall hold their offices during good behavior," and it could easily be conceived that the decision making in Rowe versus Wade was anything but "good behavior" for the judges who voted in the affirmative, a decision that has cost the lives of literally millions of unborn babies. Furthermore, their is nothing in the Bill of Rights or the subsequent amendments that affords any reasonable interpretation of a woman being given the choice of whether to preserve or spare the life of her unborn child.

But it is the law of the land, and we live with it until some more reasonable and morally responsible members of Administration, Congress or the Court itself take steps to remedy the 1972 decision.

17

Steps taken by pro-life activists have received set backs here in our country, although reasonable, non-violent demonstrations should be protected by our First Amendment. And it should go without saying that violent acts of the pro-life activists are not justified and should be handled in our courts of law.

Homosexuality

Now we come to an arena where much has been said, but a lot more needs to be proclaimed. I approach this subject with respect, because the majority of the persons caught up in this lifestyle honestly believe that they are inherently homosexual, and not because they have simply chosen that lifestyle.

Even a prominent psychiatric association in the United States is said to have the authority to discipline its members should they make attempts to change the lifestyle of a homosexual to heterosexual. But the truth is that all sexual behavior is by choice. No one coming into this world is born homosexual. I have great empathy for those who have been confirmed in their belief that somehow they have been singled out by their Creator, if they believe in one, to be a misunderstood homosexual.

The homosexual folk I have been in contact with are mostly talented, sensitive people. But because of their lifestyle they usually suffer from many forms of rejection. Often they feel misunderstood, hated and sometimes learn to hate themselves, and spiral into a suicidal depression.

Why am I so sure that people are not born that way? First, our own anatomy tells us that God did not create us to be sexually joined in any meaningful way. Second, the Bible makes it very clear that one of the results of disregarding God as Creator, and not giving thanks to him, and not glorifying him as God, is that "God gave them over to the sinful desires of their hearts to sexual impurity for the degrading of their bodies with one another."[1] This is taken from Paul's letter to the Roman church, and the verses that follow are even more descriptive, "God gave them over to shameful lusts. Even their women exchanged natural relations for unnatural ones. In the same way the men also abandoned natural relations with women and were inflamed with lust for one another."[2]

Changing ones behavior from homosexual to heterosexual in itself is not positive. What is positive is to come to realize that God created mankind male and female, that they should be joined in marriage and produce offspring. Sexuality is God given. It is not only for procreation but also for the expression of the deepest love relationships. But those deep sexual love relationships are to be confined to the sanctity of marriage. The writer of the Hebrews said it this way, "Marriage should be honored by all, and the marriage bed kept pure, for God will judge the adulterer and all the sexually immoral."[3]

We live in a day of homosexual activism with "gay pride" parades, demands for special treatment, marriage "rights," and the list goes on.

Often homosexual couples are given adoption privileges. Bills are presented to our legislative bodies to accomplish vast changes in our social laws in regard to the homosexual lifestyle. School curriculum is often being adapted to orient our children about how homosexual people live and teach them to accept the homosexual lifestyle as normal.

Not many years ago a minister caught in the homosexual lifestyle was defrocked. Today, in denomination after denomination, church bodies are being urged to ordain openly homosexual ministers.

And all of this in the face of many clear statements in the Bible about the subject. The description of homosexual behavior is not only found in the first chapter of Romans. The story of Sodom, (from which we get our word "sodomizing") and Gomorrah, and the prohibition of homosexuality in the laws of Moses, are two examples that lead us to believe that God did not intend for any of his people to be homosexual.

If there is any question about the Sodom and Gomorrah story it is recapitulated in the book of Jude: "In a similar way, Sodom and Gomorrah and the surrounding towns gave themselves up to sexual immorality and perversion."[4]

Now let's look at the health factor. HIV and Aids probably did not originate with male homosexuals in America. But whether or not that is the source, the fact remains that most of the disease comes through homosexual men. Aids research and new medicines have given some relief, but wouldn't one think that when a lifestyle is reducing life expectancy to less than 40 years, as it was a few years ago, that one would question the lifestyle? But that didn't happen in America. Instead, since the inception of Aids, homosexual activism has increased, but with loud cries for Aids help and research.

When we oppose changes in our laws to benefit homosexual men and women, we are called homophobic. When we resist the strong educational movement to train our children to accept the lifestyle as normal we are accused of hate. I have no fear and I do not hate any of them. I am just sorry that so many have honestly believed that God intended them to be that way and pray that many would join the ranks of hundreds who have come out of the lifestyle, because they believed it was not honoring to their Creator.

It is not wrong for a man to love another man. A good example in the Bible is the relationship of David with the son of King Saul, Jonathan. It used to be that men or women would live together for the main purpose of comradeship and saving on housing expenses. Today, when two of the same sex live together it is almost immediately assumed that they are homosexual. This assumption is unfortunate.

And for persons to feel sexual feelings about their own nudity, or with others of the same sex in a locker room, again is not a sign that somehow they are homosexual.

Bisexual, Transvestite and Transgender

Bisexual is a term that is applied to a person who is attracted to both sexes, usually meaning that they engage in sexual activity with both genders. There are too many tragic stories of how families have been torn apart because of one of the partners engaging in this kind of activity. Again, all sexual activity is by choice. God made us with sexual glands and organs. God made

us with the ability to have deep satisfaction in loving relationships with our spouses. But his condemnation against all forms of
sexual immorality are clearly set forth in the Bible.

There is also in our culture today a kind of "anything goes"
attitude.

The transvestite is one who enjoys dressing and seeking to
act out the behavior of the opposite sex. Some would advocate
the encouragement of this behavior. To others it is just disgusting,
and should not be condoned or encouraged.

Then there are an increasing number who have had operations to change their gender—sometimes called "trans-gender."
To anyone contemplating such a change, I would only caution
that the greatest satisfactions come in life when we accept the
condition and role God has given us and ask his guidance in living out that role.

The sexual revolution has indeed transformed our society,
but definitely not for the good. Families have been torn apart.
Children have been brought up with emotional scars There has
been no clear direction for the teenagers Millions of innocent,
unborn children, have had their short existence terminated.
Meanwhile, we sit back and watch the media announce the "Gay
Pride Parade," while our children are taught to be tolerant, with a
new meaning for the word and prompted in determining their
own clarification of values.

Endnotes

1. Romans 1:24 (NIV)
2. Romans 1:26-27 (NIV
3. Hebrews 13:4 (NIV)
4. Jude 7 (NIV)

Chapter Three

THE ENVIRONMENT

Rather than beginning our discussion of the environment at the level of the preservation of the fringe-toed lizard or the spotted owl, let us make some general observations about our environment, and then look specifically at various facets of the subject.

To live in the modern world it should be easily apparent that the preservation of our environment is essential. Pollution caused by the carelessness of industry or unthinking individuals is of concern to us all. We don't like to see our beaches polluted with sewage so that bathers are not allowed to swim until the pollution level is diminished. It's not pleasant to breathe on a day that the smog level is extremely high. We object to "litter bugs" that make highways and parks unsightly. Most of us care about our environment, at least in so far as our own health, safety and enjoyment are concerned.

Where the disagreement comes is where concern for environmental issues overshadows the freedom or sovereignty of a nation or the individual's freedom to utilize his own property, especially when the scientific evidence is not conclusive.

Following the Industrial Revolution, opportunities for pollution greatly increased. And in America, as the population increased so did the need to preserve our surroundings. In 1907 the first Chief of the U. S. Forest Service was appointed, Gifford Pinchot. The idea of the Service was to control nature and serve the material interests of mankind. Our Bureau of Reclamation, concerning itself with building dams, also followed this same general philosophy, that is, to use and preserve nature for the benefit of mankind. A half a century later a new breed of environmentalists began to emerge that challenged the original philosophy, believing that components of nature have an inherent value in themselves, not related to the benefit of mankind.

Caring about nature and being kind to animals was not in itself a new concept. Ancient writings reveal such respect for the environment and living things. One individual who left his mark on the thinking of succeeding generations was Henry David Thoreau, who made his famous departure to Walden Pond in 1845. He was a naturalist philosopher who saw so much to celebrate in nature, while he withdrew from his fellow man for a time. He stated an axiom, "every creature is better alive than dead, men and moose and pine trees."[1]

John Muir was another who made an impact on the thinking of America regarding the environment. One of his statements about alligators was that they were filling a "place assigned them by the greater Creator of us all" and "beautiful in the eyes of God."[2] He considered one his greatest political achievements the establishing of Yosemite National Park in California.

Albert Sweitzer's ideas came to the United States in English translations of his books in the 1920's and 1930's. Among other ideas, he espoused the concept of a reverence for all of life and all matter on earth. In 1923 he stated "Today it is thought an exaggeration to state that a reasonable ethic demands constant consideration for all living things down to the lowliest manifestations of life."[3]

Throughout the twentieth century myriad writers and organizers of right's groups have emerged, many making a great impact on the thinking of today's society. Let us delineate some of these concerns and see if we can determine where the truth really lies.

Animal Rights

In the fourth century B.C, the Greek philosopher *Aristotle* wrote that nature "made all animals for the sake of man."[4] In the biblical account of creation in Genesis we are told that God said to man, "Rule over the fish of the sea and the birds of the air and over every living creature that moves on the ground."[5]

Throughout the Middle Ages animals did not receive a lot of compassion since far more attention was being given to people who were struggling with plague and famine. As late as 1780, philosopher Immanuel Kant said, "Animals are not self-conscious, and are there merely as a means to an end. That end is man."[6]

In 1776 in England, the Reverend Humphrey Primatt wrote, "A dissertation on the Duty of Mercy and Sin of Cruelty to Brute Animals."[7] This treatise was followed by several attempts to pass laws that emphasized a more benevolent attitude toward animals. But it was not until 1824 that the Society for the Prevention of Cruelty to Animals was formed. Humane societies and other groups that favored humane treatment to animals became prominent.

Objection to experiments on live animals followed. It was called vivisection and anti-vivisection groups became active. By the early 1900's the United States had become active in experimentation on animals. Anti-vivisection groups protested but between physicians and medical societies efforts to legally ban the practice were unsuccessful.

About this time research on germs and bacteria was coming alive. And it was research on live dogs that proved vital in the work of one Louis Pasteur. Vaccines that followed were to prove successful against rabies, diphtheria and other diseases.

By the 1960's there was growing concern about the quality of life on the planet earth. Almost a century after the writings of Darwin, the distance between humankind and animals was narrowing. Animal rights groups were forming and the concepts were varied, some feeling that animals needed liberation from human oppression. A law had been passed, The Humane Slaughter Act of 1958, which attempted to eliminate needless suffering in the killing of livestock. But activist groups were destined to be formed which would carry animal rights concepts far beyond what anyone had previously imagined.

Doris Day declared that "killing an animal to make a coat is a sin...we have no right to do it." Jayne Meadows added that nobody could wear real fur "without feeling, literally, like a murderer."[8] Greenpeace and other groups emerged in the 1970's and extended the ideas of animal rights much further. Protection of seals, whales and all sorts of creatures were included in their agendas. One of the groups, The Animal Liberation Front, made a raid against the University of California's Riverside campus in 1985, resulting in the release of 467 animals and the destruction of equipment worth $680,000. In 1987, at the University of California in Davis, The Front allegedly burned down an animal-research building valued at $2.5 million dollars.[9] Attacks continue against furriers, research operations and other industry in the name of animal rights.

Just the other day 40 some Pilot Whales were beached at Cape Cod, Massachusetts. Professionals hurried out to rescue the mammals, as millions viewed the event on television and hundreds watched from the shoreline. This kind of concern by the masses seems warranted. Concern for God's creatures seems in keeping with respect for the God who made them, and good stewardship of the environment in which he has placed us. The concern is the extreme positions that place the value of creature life even beyond that of mankind. This leads us to our next consideration.

Endangered Species

The United States passed The Endangered Species Act of 1973. The law seemed reasonable, because of the many ways modern man has polluted his environment causing the suffering and death of a variety of species. Nature also plays a part in the suffering and death of species, as in the case of forest fires caused by lightening or as in conditions of drought.

But we have gone too far. The most current example in my hemisphere is the allocation of 1000 acres of prime desert land made into a preserve for something known as a fringed-toed lizard. Hardly anyone in this valley, let alone in our country, have ever seen or ever will see a fringed-toed lizard. Meanwhile thousands of residents are suffering from unnecessary air pollution and the piling up of sand in swimming pools, patios and filtering into every nook and cranny of their homes.

The setting aside of one million acres for the Spotted Owl is another flagrant example of going far beyond reason in trying to preserve creatures, regardless of the difficulties it has caused residents who make their living from the area where the creature supposedly makes his habitat.

The truth is that God's creatures quite easily adjust their habitat when required to do so, because of forces of nature or the work of humankind. But beyond these considerations is the pronouncement of what has been taking place as told by the Apostle Paul in the Bible, in Romans chapter one. He was relating a universal condition of mankind, but the chapter so vividly describes what has been taking place in dramatic form, especially in the last half-century. He describes man as having had the opportunity of beholding God's handiwork in nature, but in spite of knowing him through nature man has not honored him or been thankful for all he has been given in nature. He speaks of "foolish hearts" being "darkened and although claiming to be wise, actually becoming fools. [10]

And then he speaks about "exchanging the glory of the immortal God for images made to look like mortal man and birds and animals and reptiles." [11] In Paul's day he was referring to idol worship. Today some cultures still make images and worship them, but in our day man has done the same thing through evolution. He has exhalted God's creatures above God himself. Paul puts it like this: "They exchanged the truth of God for a lie, and worshiped and served created things rather than the Creator." [12]

Should we care about endangered species? Of course. But where we have gone today with the concept in case after case, is outside the boundaries of reason and not in keeping with the position God intended for us in monitoring our planet.

Global Warming and Air Pollution

Our memories seem quite short. In very recent history, scientists concluded that from 1940 to the mid-70's, average northern hemispheric temperatures dipped by a fraction of a degree Centigrade. [13] Lowell Ponte was one of the many scientists who believed that the earth was cooling rapidly and wrote "The Cooling," published in 1976.[14] The April 28, 1975 edition of Newsweek reported that "There are ominous signs that the earth's weather patterns have begun to change dramatically and that these changes may portend a drastic decline in food production—with serious political implications for just about every nation on earth." Peter Gwynne was responsible for this statement.[15]

Now, only 27 years later, some scientists and politicians have pressed the issue of global warming until a large part of the world's population has been made to fear that global warming is such a reality that drastic earth changes could endanger life on the planet.

The reality is that reputable scientists are divided on the subject. A slight rise in world temperature over recent years appears to be a fact. The question is whether these variations—slight cooling from 1940 to the mid-70;s and now ever so slight warming—are natural phenomena or whether the industrialized nations are actually contributing to the changes.

The key phrase is "greenhouse gases." Yes, the earth's atmosphere amounts to a "greenhouse" effect. All the earth's heat comes from the radiation of the sun. We are told that a fraction of the heat that comes to the earth goes into the atmosphere as infrared radiation. And that we are told contributes to further warming by being absorbed by particles of air called "greenhouse gases." These gases are primarily carbon dioxide, methane, hydrocarbons, aerosols and last but not least—water. And water is responsible for 98 percent of greenhouse warming.

Apparently the Greenhouse theory that an increase in the concentration of any of the greenhouse gases will lead to increased warming is not disputed. The question is whether the changes caused by industrialization or other activities of mankind have a significant role in the process. Over the past 100 years an increase of no more than one half of one degree Centigrade has been accounted for.[15]

Then there is the fact that nature itself seems to cause unaccountable changes. Although records are not available certain events in history indicate some of the changes. When the Vikings crossed the North Atlantic Ocean there were no icebergs and they named their newfound discovery "Greenland." It was green at that time, but today it is covered with glacial ice. Many other examples show that warming and cooling is a constant pattern of nature.

Another fact to consider is that far more carbon dioxide is produced by natural phenomena—such as volcanoes—than by human activity.

Quite recently in the State of California, legislation was passed to cause auto manufacturers to alter auto engines, and a primary selling point was the change it would bring in the "greenhouse effect." Air pollution seemed secondary.

Global warming is an unresolved issue. However, it came to a head for our world at the United Nations Conference on Environment and Development. This "Global Forum" was attended by upwards of 20,000 participants from around the world. It took place in Rio de Janeiro, Brazil in June of 1992. The serious work that came out of the conference was done at what was called "Earth Summit" and 178 nations were represented.

Out of the Earth Summit came "The Global Climate Change Treaty." This was an international treaty and it was signed by President George Bush and ratified by the United States Senate on October 15, 1992.

Unfortunately, an international treaty becomes the law of the land and overrides domestic law. It is estimated that this treaty will be enormously expensive to the United States in days to come. And it is all based on a highly questionable premise with which many leading scientists did not agree.

On June 1, 1992, 250 of the world's leading scientists, including 27 Nobel laureates, released a statement called the Heidelberg Appeal. In part this statement read, "We are worried, at the dawn of the 21st Century, at the emergence of an irrational ideology which is opposed to scientific and industrial progress and impedes economic and social development...The greatest evils which stalk our Earth are ignorance and oppression, and Science, Technology, and Industry, whose instruments, when adequately managed, are indispensable tools of a future shaped by Humanity, by itself and for itself, overcoming major problems like overpopulation, starvation, and worldwide diseases."[16]

Some day the United States may be gravely sorry about entering into this global treaty, since the direction of the treaty is to radically change the industrialization in the United States and have the United States accept the largest portion of financial responsibility in modifying the "Greenhouse effect."

Air pollution, on the other hand, is a very legitimate concern, and a very serious one. Recently in one nation, air pollution was so concentrated and toxic that a number of deaths occurred and much of the population resorted to face masks of one kind or another. Here in the United States air quality testing and control has been in progress over the last several decades, with some success.

To continuously monitor, test and control air pollution world-wide is rational and indeed urgently needed. Concern for global warming on the other hand should be just that—a concern. World famed scientists do not agree that human effort will make any significant impact on global warming. History tells us that for centuries there have been modifications in the earth's temperature due to many unknown causes. It is now a major political issue throughout the world and it appears it will be in some generations to come—perhaps until a slight world temperature drop is again observed.

But what is so amazing is this. The proponents of the theory of global warming are so concerned over the possible effects of that warming on the planet during the next several decades or even a hundred years. Yet many of them also embrace the theory of evolution. If they believe the planet to be in the hundreds of millions of years old, how do they suppose the earth has kept its temperature under control without man's help over all those years?

The truth is "The earth is the Lord's, and everything in it, the world, and all who live in it; for he founded it upon the seas and established it upon the waters."[17] Or as the song put it, "He's got the whole world in His hands."

Good stewardship over the environment God has placed us in—that makes sense. Kindness to creatures He placed on earth—that goes almost without saying. But we are not to worship and serve created things rather than the Creator. And on global warming, we should be satisfied with continued research, rather than making a political issue out of it and bringing fear to the world population.

Endnotes

1. Nash, Roderick, *The Rights of Nature,* Madison, Wisconsin: The University of Wisconsin Press, 1989, page 37.

2. *Ibid.,* page 39.

3. *Ibid.,* page 62.

4. Pringle, Lawrence, *The Animal Rights Controversy,* Orlando, Florida: Harcourt Brace Jovanovich, 1989, page 4.

5. Genesis 1:28 (NIV)

6. Pringle, Lawrence, *The Animal Rights Controversy,* Orlando, Florida: Harcourt Brace Jovanovich, 1989, page 6.

7. *Ibid.,* page 6.

8. Nash, Roderick, *The Rights of Nature,* Madison, Wisconsin: The University of Wisconsin Press, 1989, page 183.

9. *Ibid.,* page 189.

10. Romans 1:21-22 (NIV)

11. Romans 1:23 (NIV)

12. Romans 1:25 (NIV)

13. Ray, Dixie Lee and Guzzo, Louis R, *Environmental Overkill,* Washington, D. C.: Regnery Gateway, 1993, page 14-15.

14. *Ibid.,* page 14.

15. *Ibid.,* page 18

16. *Ibid.,* page 6-7

17. Psalms 24:1 (NIV)

Chapter Four

THE INVISIBLE WALL

This chapter is about the founding of the United States, it's Constitution and Bill of Rights. For those of you reading it in another country, it will clarify some misgivings you may have heard about our country and it may also help you identify the concepts of freedom and apply them to your own country.

But to all of you who are citizens of our beloved United States of America, you will want to pay close attention to our history and not be swayed by the revisions of history or the false concept of the meaning of separation between church and state.

A good place to start in looking at the history of the United States of America, is that stalwart group of pioneers who crossed the Atlantic on a ship called "The Mayflower." A good way to understand what they were about is to look at the historic "Mayflower Compact," written on November 11, 1620. They purposed "...to plant the first colonie in the Northerne parts of Virginia." But their bravery and determination can hardly be understood without looking at the entire compact:

> "In the name of God, Amen. We whose names are under-written, the loyall subjects of our dread soveraigne Lord, King James, by the grace of God, of Great Britaine, France, and Ireland king, defender of the faith, etc., Having undertaken for the gloire of God, and advance-ments of the Christian faith, and honour of our king and countrie, a voyage to plant the first colonie in the Northerne parts of Virginia, doe by these presents solemnly and mutually in the presence of God, and one of another, covenant and combine ourselves togeather into a civil body politick..."

Most important in the minds of these pioneers was obviously establishing a colony where God would be acknowledged and the Christian faith advanced. But as Dr. Bob Dugan pointed out in his book, "Stand and Be Counted," one of the publishers of a high school history textbook, Harcourt, Brace, Jovanovich, in 1986 provided a version of that compact by leaving out every reference to God and the Christian faith.[1] The true meaning and the motivation of those Pilgrim fathers was of course lost, and students were given a false impression of this aspect of the founding of our nation. Unfortunately that is only one example of history revision that has engulfed our textbooks and deprived our children from knowing the real truth about America and her roots.

Many years passed before the colonists felt that strong, united need to resist the tyranny of the king of their beloved homeland. But the recognition of a sovereign God over the affairs of men was still in place. Samuel Adams expressed it well in a poem:

> All temporal power is of God,
> And the magistratal, His institution, laud,
> To but advance creaturely happiness aubaud:
> Let us then affirm the Source of Liberty.
> Ever agreeable to the nature and will,
> Of the Supreme and Guardian of all yet still
> Employed for our rights and freedom's thrill:
> Thus proves the only Source of Liberty.
> Though our civil joy is surely expressed
> Through hearth, and home, and church manifest,
> Yet this too shall be a nation's true test:
> To acknowledge the divine Source of Liberty.[2]

On June 9, 1776, the Continental Congress accepted a resolution of Virginia delegate Richard Henry Lee to appoint a committee to draft a declaration of secession from the dominions of the English king and Parliament.[3] The revolution had already been under way for more than a year. Then on June 29, 1776 the committee, composed of Thomas Jefferson, John Adams, Benjamin Franklin, Roger Sherman and Robert Livingston, presented their draft for debate and vote.

By July 4, 1776 an amended version was accepted.

From the very beginning it was quite clear that what was being undertaken was for the freedom of the colonists, but always in recognition of their God and Creator.

The first part of that Declaration is quite familiar to many:

"When in the course of human events, it becomes necessary for one people to dissolve the political bands which have connected them with another, and to assume among the powers of the earth the separate and equal station to which the laws of nature and of nature's God entitle them, a decent respect to the opinions of mankind requires that they should declare the causes which impel them to the separation.

"We hold these truths to be self-evident: that all men are created equal, that they are endowed by their Creator with certain unalienable rights, that among these are life, liberty, and the pursuit of happiness..."

This introduction alone sets the stage for the recognition of God, but that recognition is further reinforced in the closing paragraph, where we read, "...appealing to the Supreme Judge of the world for the rectitude of our intentions..." and, "...And for the support of this declaration, with a firm reliance on the protection of Divine Providence, we mutually pledge to each other our lives, our fortunes, and our sacred honor."

From time to time I read letters to the editor on our Opinion Page of the local newspaper. Quite a number of them give the opinion that our founding fathers set up a secular state with a clear separation between church and state. Either they have not studied the documents of our founding fathers or they have been caught up in the revision of our history, or they simply have a strong desire to leave God out of the equation.

There were no atheists affixing their names to those early documents of American history. Of course they were not all of the same religious persuasions, but respect for the Creator and Sovereign Lord was apparent. And many of them were professing and practicing Christians.

The United States had functioning governments as early as September 4, 1774, but operated as a federated nation from July 4, 1776. It would be nearly 15 years before the United States would inaugurate it's first president under the Constitution of the United States, which occurred on April 30, 1789. During that nearly 15 year period, the Continental Congress and the Confederation Congress governed the country and fourteen presidents were recognized as head of state until George Washington was elected and inaugurated under the new Constitution.

Originally a constitutional convention was convened on May 25, 1787 to amend the Articles of Confederation, with representatives from seven states. But eventually they determined that a new document would be necessary. By September 17, 1787, twelve state delegations contributed to the draft. It required ratification by nine states and due to opposition did not become official until June 21, 1788. Then by May 29, 1790 all 13 states had ratified the document.

The preamble to the Constitution is familiar to many:

> "We the people of the united States, in order to form a more perfect union, establish justice, insure domestic tranquillity, provide for the common defense, promote the general welfare, and secure the blessings of liberty to ourselves and our posterity, do ordain and establish this Constitution for the United States of America."

What follows are seven articles describing a representative form of government with checks and balances. In article six the statement is made that "...no religious test shall ever be required as a qualification to any office or public trust under the United States."

Because there was opposition to the adoption of the Constitution, especially by the anti-Federalists, several states proposed amending the Constitution for better protection for states and individuals. Thus we have the "Bill of Rights," the first ten amendments to the Constitution. Through the years others were added making to date, twenty-seven amendments.

The first amendment, termed Article I, is the one that has received the most notoriety, especially during the last half century. That article states:

"Congress shall make no law respecting an establishment of religion, or prohibiting the free exercise thereof; or abridging the freedom of speech, or of the press; or the right of the people peaceably to assemble, and to petition the government for a redress of grievances."

An establishment of religion

It should be very clear that our founding fathers were very aware of the religious history in Europe. They did not want their newly founded government to have authority over their religious life. They did not want a "state controlled" church.

Today in America that simple phrase, "establishment of religion," has been used in case after case to imply that no vestige of religion is to be in evidence where government buildings or dollars are involved. This was clearly not the intent of the founders. The Ten Commandments were displayed on public buildings. Cities, towns and streets were named after biblical places and concepts, as in Salem, (Peace) Massachusetts and Philadelphia, Pennsylvania (the city of brotherly love). Chaplains were appointed to the military and congressional houses. Oaths were taken by placing hands on the Bible.

Then where and when did we acquire the concept of "separation of church and state?" It is not in that first amendment. It was not in the practice of our founding fathers. It was first mentioned in a letter by Thomas Jefferson to the Danbury Baptists in Connecticut in 1802, fully 11 years after the Bill of Rights was ratified. He used the phrase "a wall of separation between church and state." Certainly there were varying opinions as to what that should mean. James Madison, for example took considerable exception to Jefferson's concept of church and state. But Thomas Jefferson himself had no such idea that this invisible wall would be interpreted as the ACLU (American Civil Liberties Union) and numerous American judges are interpreting it today. And again, please note that the concept was nowhere to be found in the Declaration of Independence, the Constitution or in the Bill of Rights.

While Thomas Jefferson was Superintendent of Schools in Washington, the Bible and a book by Isaac Watts, the hymn writer, were used as textbooks. And while he was in office as president he frequently attended Christian worship services in the Capitol building.

In other ways too, Jefferson gave public encouragement to Christianity and Christian morality. In his first inaugural address in 1801 he declared,

> "...enlightened by a benign religion professed, indeed, and practiced in various forms, yet all of the inculcating honesty, truth, temperance, gratitude, and the love of man; acknowledging and adoring an overruling Providence, which by all its dispensations proves that it delights in the happiness of man here and his greater happiness hereafter—with all these blessings, what more is necessary to make us a happy and prosperous people? Still one thing more, fellow citizens—a wise and frugal Government, which shall restrain men from injuring one another, shall leave them otherwise free to regulate their own pursuits of industry and improvement, and shall not take from the mouth of labor the bread it has earned. This is the sum of good government, and this is necessary to close the circle of our felicities."[4]

Now let's go back to our First Congress. Nothing in their behavior suggested any alienation of Christianity or Christian symbols from their political life. Indeed that First Congress made a Christian worship service part of the inauguration of George Washington as first president of the United States under the Constitution. On April 27, 1789, the United States Senate made such a resolution, followed two days later by the House of Representatives. "This official service was conducted by the Right Reverend Samuel Provost, who had been elected as Chaplain of Congress on April 29, 1789. The service was held in St. Paul's Chapel, an Episcopal church. The President, the Vice-President, and all the members of the House and the Senate attended the service. Washington solemnly took his oath of office, kissed the Bible upon which he had placed his hand while the oath had been administered, and read his obviously Christian inaugural address."[5]

The most notable change in the meaning and application of that first phrase in the First Amendment was when Justice Hugo Black, in 1947, brought out the concept of the "wall of separation" in Everson versus the Board of Education of Ewing Township. That "establishment clause" was then interpreted to mean that government is prohibited from aiding all religions.

Today separation of church and state arguments are made as though our founding fathers established a purely secular government. Nothing could be further from the truth. The first phrase of the First Amendment simply states that Congress shall not be in the business of establishing a particular religion as the religion of the land as European states had done.

Or prohibiting the free exercise therof

The second phrase of the First Amendment is just as important. Congress shall make no law prohibiting the *free exercise* of religion. The Ten Commandments on court room walls, Bibles in schools and public libraries, prayer at football games and graduation ceremonies are all part of the free exercise of religion. To our founding fathers that was essentially the Christian religion. As a matter of record the United States Supreme Court made this declaration in 1892:

> "Our laws and our institutions must necessarily be based upon the teachings of the Redeemer of Mankind. It is impossible that it should be otherwise; and in this sense and to this extent, our civilization and our institutions are emphatically Christian."

There is nothing in the First Amendment that would indicate that our founding fathers wanted a purely secular society, or that the Bill of Rights was set up to protect atheists or minority religions from being offended by an essentially Christian society.

During the Dwight David Eisenhower administration several things were done to reinforce our dependence upon God as a nation:

1952   A National Day of Prayer was declared. (This was not a new concept, as many previous presidents from Washington on down had declared days of prayer and thanksgiving to God.)

1954   A Joint Resolution of Congress to place the words "under God" in the Pledge of Allegiance.

1955   "In God We Trust" was required on every piece of our money.

1956   "In God We Trust" became our national motto.

Recently in America, our 11th Circuit Court of Appeals, a liberal court, declared that students in many Western states could not recite the Pledge of Allegiance because it contained the words "under God."

Once again we have had liberal judges applying their own rules for our society, completely ignoring our origins and the foundation of our society. Meanwhile, dozens of nominations to federal judgeships have been held up in our senate because our current president, George W. Bush, has nominated conservative individuals to these offices, ones who will not be likely to support the onslaught of the ACLU in their attempt to remove every vestige of Christianity from public life.

Long ago a nation that had been established and blessed by God, chose to go their own way and Jeremiah the prophet was the one who spoke it and put it in writing:

> "My people have committed two sins: They have forsaken me, the spring of living water, and have dug their own cisterns, broken cisterns that can hold no water."[6]

It appears that America is taking the same path. No, we don't need mandated religion. That never works. But we do need the freedom of religious expression. Freedom of religion is needed, not freedom from religion.

Since our awful tragedy of September 11, 2001 in New York, Washington, D. C., and Pennsylvania, we as a nation have brought out our flags and declared our support for our country, singing and posting signs and placards, "God bless America." But how can we expect God to bless America when America does not appear ready to bless God, or even allow him in the class-room or the courthouse?

Endnotes

1. Dugan, Robert, *Stand and Be Counted,* Sisters, Oregon: Multnomah Books, 1995, pages 82-83.

2. Grant, George, *The Pocket Patriot,* Nashville, Tennessee: Cumberland House, 2000, page 40.

3. *Ibid.*, page 41.

4. Kennedy, D. James, *Reclaiming the Lost Legacy,* Fort Lauderdale, Florida, Coral Ridge Ministries, page 46.

5. *Ibid.*, page 43.

6. Isaiah 2:13 (NIV)

Chapter Five

A DEFINING MOMENT

September 11, 2001 has changed forever the world in which we live. On that day 19 men from several divergent nations took upon themselves the responsibility of teaching the United States of America a lesson. At the cost of their own lives they hijacked four commercial airlines and piloted two of them into the World Trade Center Towers in New York City, one of them into the Pentagon building in Washington, D. C., and one crashed in a wooded area of Pennsylvania, due to the courageous intervention of the passengers. All crew members and passengers lost their lives along with several thousand innocent occupants of the World Trade Center buildings and the Pentagon. Included in the casualties were hundreds of firefighters and police officers.

Today we remember it as "Ground Zero" in New York City. It is a hole, seven stories beneath the surface of the ground where the Trade Center buildings once stood. We've past our remembrance of the first anniversary of that awful event. But we will never lose the effect of that tragic day.

On that day, our newly elected President, George W. Bush, a God-fearing man, formerly Governor of Texas, led our nation to recognize that we were at war. This time it was a war without geographical boundaries. It was a war against terrorism. It was a war against evil. The predominant leader of that evil tyranny was known as Osama Ben Ladin, who for years had been conducting training camps for terrorists. The group is known as El Quida. Members of the group hale from various countries around the world. Over the past year a number of them have been killed in war in Afghanistan conducted by the United States and several allied countries. Others have been driven into hiding. The Taliban government of Afghanistan has been defeated. But the threat of terrorism continues to be a worldwide concern, and will continue to be long into the foreseeable future.

Economic Changes

The immediate effect of the terrorist attack of September 11 was felt on Wall Street. Airlines were in jeopardy and could see no solution without large government support. Hundreds of industries felt the blow and large layoffs became common. Retirement accounts shriveled since most of them depended heavily on the sagging stock market.

Then right in midst of these woes, a very large company, Enron, was accused of manipulating energy prices as well as giving enormous bonuses to top executives as the company was going down—millions of dollars that should have gone to stock holders and retirement accounts. Meanwhile, faulty bookkeeping made it appear that the company was worth billions of dollars more than actual value. And the corruption scandals didn't stop here. World Com, that owned MCI, was caught in similar apparent misuse of funds as well as juggling the books to deceive stockholders. Other companies were falling prey to similar schemes, and in the center of the ring was one of the largest accounting firms that had long been trusted by American business.

What followed was legal proceedings against some of America's top executives and new legislation attempting to control the greed of corporate executives. And all of this adding to the diminishing trust in America's economic condition.

Political Posturing

Overall citizen approval of the President's actions since September 11 have been very high, but strong political posturing has been continuing at the same time. We are in an election year and the control of the two houses of Congress is a much sought after prize. At the present time the Republicans have the majority in the House of Representatives by a small margin and the Democrats have a one vote lead in the Senate.

41

The Democratic platforms will undoubtedly concentrate on the economy, a strong point in past campaigns. And of course they will do their best to show a superior posture on the war against terrorism.

However, one of the most disturbing aspects of the behavior of some of the Democrats is their opposition to the efforts of President Bush to place strong, godly men and women in places of leadership. It was frightful to listen to the diatribes against John Ashcroft when he was nominated for Attorney General. I was appalled at the bashing of Mr. Ashcroft by my own California Senator Feinstein. And Senator Tom Daschle has been a persistent roadblock as majority leader in the Senate. Our president has sent dozens of names of outstanding nominees for federal judgeships, only to have them held up in committee or turned down because of their stand on abortion or other issues. Meanwhile, Chief Justice William Rehnquist quite recently asked Congress for 54 more judgeships.

Religious Posturing

When we celebrated the one year anniversary of September 11, the flags were flying again in larger numbers, the "God bless America" banners were more visible and the pulpits of America echoed more national pride and prayers for the blessing of America. But again, how can we expect God to bless America, until once again America blesses God? When God is allowed back in the classroom—when voluntary prayer is okay at school—when God's creation is recognized for what it is—and not an accidental falling out from millions of years of evolution—when Christmas is freely celebrated in schools and public places—when the Ten Commandments are back on the courtroom walls—when abortion is recognized for what it is, the killing of innocent, unborn babies—when sexual morality is recognized in the land—when America returns to the principles of its founding fathers.

The Apostle Paul in writing to the Roman church declared that "the authorities that exist have been established by God."[1] It was a passage designed to urge Christian citizens to be law abiding where possible, no matter who may be in power over the country. But it is especially significant for America. From its beginning, the United States of America has been a blessed nation—today the most powerful nation in the world and the most sought after as the country in which to live. But all this could change—through nuclear or biological warfare, natural disasters or other events. We would do well to heed the advice given by God to King Solomon when he finished building the temple long ago, "if my people, who are called by my name, will humble themselves and pray and seek my face and turn from their wicked ways, then will I hear from heaven and will forgive their sin and will heal their land."[2]

Endnotes

1. Romans 13:1 (NIV)
2. II Chronicles 7:14 (NIV)

Chapter Six

WHAT ARE WE TEACHING
OUR CHILDREN?

I went to the Desert Sands Unified School District in La Quinta, California, not far from my home. I was curious about the text books being used in that rather large school district, and what was being taught about our history as a nation, and what was being presented in science.

As I perused the textbooks for elementary school children on our history, I was rather pleased to find that a very thorough account was given about the Pilgrims coming over on the Mayflower and a very accurate account of the Mayflower Compact was cited, including the entire text with all the references to God. From that point the history was delineated in detail, even telling of The Great Awakening in our early history. No attempt seemed to be made to eliminate references to God, in contrast to the reference made earlier in Chapter Four to a publication for our schools by Harcourt, Brace, Jovanovich in 1986, in which all references to the name of God were left out in the reciting of the Mayflower Compact.

It was a very different story when I came to the textbooks on science for the seventh graders. Here in a textbook by Prentice Hall I read that "earth's history goes back 4.6 billion years."[1] It was simply presented as a known scientific fact, along with a delineation of earth's history:

"end of the last ice age	10,000 years
whales evolve	50,000,000 years
Pangaea begins to break up	225,000,000 years
first vertebrates develop	530,000,000 years

multicellular ...develop (algae)	1,000,000,000 years
first life (bacteria)	3,500,000,000 years
oldest knowns rock forms	4,000,000,000 years
age of the earth	4,600,000,000 years [2]

Then there were pages and pages teaching the youngsters that the earth and all living things came about by the process of evolution. Sophisticated words like "gradualism" and "punctuated equilibria"[3] were used to explain some of the difficulties of the explanation. The use of radioisotopes in dating things was explained along with a picture of a scientist using a dating machine. In fact there were dozens of elaborate color pictures used to tell the story of earth, life and man. All of it was presented as fact and science.

Of course the big problem is that what was presented is only the view of some scientists. It is evolution in its rawest form. It is based on a belief system that is more of a religion than a science. It starts with the theory that all life on earth, and the earth itself, came from some place of origin other than God. In the textbooks, none of the real problems of the evolutionary theory are dealt with.

One problem scientists have been wrestling with is that if the earth has been in a state of nuclear decay for 1.5 billion years, as some are saying, then where has the helium gone that is emitted during the process? This question was brought out by Melvin Cook in 1957 in his article in *Nature*, "Where is the earth's radiogenic helium?"[4] Other scientists have continued the question and Dr. Larry Vardiman, an atmospheric scientist, has shown that even after accounting for the slow leakage in space, the earth's atmosphere has only about 0.04% of the helium it should have if the earth were billions of years old.[5]

There is currently a study going on by a group of scientists on this subject and they expect to have technical details from their study of the escaping of helium for presentation the summer of 2003. So far their findings show that the earth's age is in the thousands of years, not billions.

Unfortunately, promoters of the evolutionary theory, rush to the media with every recent finding to show the validity of teachings. For example, very recently we have been told that chimpanzees have 98% of the same DNA that humans have, and we are to be impressed that this discovery gives credence to common ancestry. But no such conclusion is within the findings of DNA research. R. J. Mural states that recent research shows just 2.5% of DNA is different between people and mice, and only 1% different from a chimpanzee."[6] And then there is the UK chief scientist who said, "We share half our genes (DNA) with the banana."[7]

So only one side of the debate is given to our children, and it is a flawed, dangerous course to travel. And what I pointed out above is only the minutia of the scientific research available, to say nothing of all of the problems of the evolutionary theory previously mentioned in Chapter One.

We are not telling our children the truth about the earth and man's origin and the results are showing up in all arenas of our society.

One major area affected, or course, is in the areas of values. Once in our educational posture, we were reasonably sure that there were some absolutes—God-given ones, like the ones in the Ten Commandments. Now we live in an age of moral relativism and there are supposedly no absolutes.

In our schools we teach something called "Values Clarification," which means little more than having the students decide what their values are and confirming them. And we teach "Tolerance." Tolerance used to be a good word to indicate our patience and understanding of other people with whom we may not agree. Today it is taught as what we might call the "New Tolerance," meaning that we not only understand but confirm and approve another's attitude or lifestyle, regardless how far it may be from what we know as moral or true.

Unfortunately the largest teachers union, the NEA (National Education Association) is a large part of the problem. George Will of the Washington Post wrote an article which appeared in our local paper at the time of our celebrating the first anniversary of the September 11 attacks. He had been observing the NEA Web site, and found more confirmation of his negative attitude toward the NEA. He stated that the recommendations of how to treat the children on this one year observance displayed three things: (1) Distrust of parents, (2) Politically correct obsession with "diversity" and America's sins, and (3) (the one Mr. Will finds most repellent) Therapeutic rather than educational focus—an emphasis not on learning but on feelings, not on good thinking, but on feeling good.[8]

The NEA had apparently asked a psychologist, Brian Lippincott, of John F. Kennedy University in California, to provide "tips for parents and teachers," such as "Use language that is developmentally appropriate for children." Added to this was the recommendation that we should be aware that "some of this country's darkest moments resulted from prejudice and intolerance for our own people." And one emphasis of September 11 should be on "historical instances of American intolerance."[9]

"The NEA says the lessons to be learned from the terrorist attacks are: 'Appreciating and getting along with people of diverse backgrounds and cultures, the importance of anger management and global awareness'."[10]

Mr. Will also commented on one other idea from the recommendations: "Give students the opportunity to discuss and have validated their feelings about the events of September 11 in a nonjudgmental discussion circle."[9] He was concerned that the children were to be taught more about there own serenity than about the their nation and its rigors in responding to the world's dangers.

Any even casual observance of what has been going on in our schools ought to alert us to the need for drastic reform in our entire educational system. Violence and guns in school classrooms, difficulty in many schools to provide discipline, low ratings on basic testing are just a few of the problems.

A classmate of mine who graduated the same year as I did from Princeton Theological Seminary, the Rev. Lou Sheldon, founder and Director of Traditional Values Coalition, did a study on some of the happenings since Christian principles began to be removed from American public life starting in 1962. In that year the Supreme Court of the United States prohibited the saying of this simple non-denominational prayer in public schools:

> "Almighty God, we acknowledge our dependence upon thee, beg thy blessings upon us, our parents, our teachers, and our country."

The following year the Supreme Court banned Bible teachings in public schools, and in 1980 ordered public schools to remove the Ten Commandments from student view.

Mr. Sheldon points out that since 1962, SAT scores are down 10 percent, on tests made easier, teen suicide is up 450 percent, illegal drugs are up 6,000 percent, criminal arrests of teens are up 150 percent, and births to unmarried girls are up 500 percent.

The correlation between what we are teaching our children and our insistence that no Godly, or Christian influence be allowed in our classroom is all too painfully obvious.

Sex education is taught, but not abstinence until marriage. Condoms are available in some school clinics. Abortions are sometimes recommended to be done without parental knowledge or consent.

The picture is dismal, but not hopeless. Many serious minded, Christian teachers are teaching in public schools. A law was passed to allow Christian groups to have the same privilege as other groups using school property for their meetings. Occasionally "60 Minutes" or other television program relates some very successful public schools where discipline is the norm, college entrance the goal for the majority and some minority students given every opportunity to achieve along with the rest of the successful students.

Voucher programs have been somewhat successful. Here the parents are permitted to enroll their children in private schools, without the usual heavy fee. Public educators usually complain about the system, but since over-crowding is often a real problem, why not let the voucher system be a method of relieving the over-crowded classroom?

By teaching the unproven theory of evolution, we have undermined the most valuable incentive children can ever have—

hope. If there is no hope, life becomes basically meaningless. If man is not created by God, but is rather the product of an evolutionary process, then he has no reason to believe he has a soul or spirit or after life. He becomes his own god and only what benefits him is good. Even benevolent acts become a means to self-enhancement.

School bonds, building new schools, providing more sophisticated computers in the classroom, and better salaries are not going to solve our basic education problems.

It is time to recognize that our forefathers had no intention of taking God out of the classroom—in fact they used Bibles as textbooks. It is time to allow voluntary prayer in school, keep "one nation, under God" in place in our pledge of allegiance and keep the Ten Commandments in public view where desirable. It is time to put the findings of creation scientists in the text books. It is time to recognize that the First Amendment to the Constitution of the United States was established to keep the government from establishing one church for the nation and controlling it, not to remove religion from the halls of education or society.

In the United States, the House of Representatives, in a vote of 401 to 5 approved the leaving of "one nation, under God" in the pledge of allegiance and keeping our nation's motto: "In God We Trust." The date of that passage, October 8, 2002. That's a good beginning. Now let's be sure our public schools know it. The Chinese proverb says, "A journey of 1000 miles begins with one step." Let's keep on with the journey.

2. Darwin, Charles. *Origin of Species.* Chicago, Illinois: Great Books, Encyclopedia Britannica, Inc., 1952, page 134-135.

Endnotes

1. Science Explorer, *Focus on Life Science,* Needham, Mass.: Prentice Hall, 2000, page 182.

2. *Ibid.*, page 183.

3. *Ibid.*, page 148.

4. Cook, Melvin A., "Where is the earth's radiogenic helium?" *Nature,* 179:213, 1957.

5. Vardiman, Larry, *The Age of the Earth's Atmosphere: A Study of the Helium Flux through the Atmosphere* (San Diego, CA: Institute for Creation Research, 1990), page 28.

6. Mural, R. J., et al., *Science,* v. 296, May 31, 2002, p. 1661.

7. May, R., Quoted in Coglan & Boyce, *New Scientist* 167 (July 1):5, 2000.

8. Will, George, *"NEA puts feel-good spin on 9-11,"* Palm Springs, CA., The Desert Sun, August 25, 2002, page B5.

9. *Ibid.*

10. *Ibid.*

Chapter Seven

WHO ARE THE PLAYERS?

The NEA

We have already indicated in our last chapter that one of the key players in what is happening in America is the NEA (The National Education Association). They are a key player because they claim to have 2.7 million members who work at every level of education. They claim to have affiliates in every state, as well as in 13,000 local communities across the United States.

The association was founded in 1857. It has as it's original mission.

> "To fulfill the promise of a democratic society, the National Education Association shall promote the cause of quality public education and advance the profession of education; expand the rights and further the interest of educational employees; and advocate human, civil, and economic rights for all."

They are a volunteer-based organization supported by a network of staff at the national level. At the local level, affiliates are active raising funds for scholarship programs, conducting professional workshops on issues that affect faculty and explore the area of bargaining contracts for school district employees.

At the state level, affiliates lobby legislators for the resources schools need, do campaigning and file legal actions to protect academic freedom.

At the national level, NEA lobbies Congress and federal agencies, supports and coordinates innovative projects, provides training and assistance to affiliates and other related activities.

They also reach out on an international level in seeking to make what they term effective schools and education.

As noble as their original mission statement sounds, the current governing body today is not moving the educational life in America in a godly or productive way. Although all of the ills of the educational system cannot be blamed on this one association, their liberal bias certainly contributes to the problem. Their attitude toward sex education, the gay and lesbian issues, Creation Science, abortion rights and prayer in school are far from ideologies that enhance their fulfilling of their original mission of providing quality education.

As noted in our last chapter, George Will's feelings about the NEA are not far from the reality that the NEA needs a complete overhaul to help bring the public school classrooms back to places of discipline, more teaching of fundamentals and less emphasis on quasi therapy sessions. SAT scores are only a measure of our failure to offer a solid education together with some reasonable hope for the future. It may sound like a cliché, but when God went out, guns came in to our classrooms. The future of our nation is dependent on the young people we are educating and the NEA is not leading us in the right direction.

The ACLU

The American Civil Liberties Union, founded in 1920, is supposed to be the nation's "guardian of liberty." They claim nearly 300,000 supporters with offices in almost every state. They have frequently appeared before federal courts and the U. S. Supreme Court.

Unfortunately, while the ACLU claims to be the guardian of individual freedom and liberty, they have used their power and strategy to come up against almost every vestige of God and Christianity in our nation, with the help of liberal judges. They have succeeded in outlawing prayer and banning God and the Ten Commandments from public schools.

They have frequently had Nativity Scenes removed from public places. They have removed the Ten Commandments from courtrooms. They have stopped Christmas pageants and the singing of Christmas carols in schools and public places. Theirs is clearly an anti-Christian, even anti-God agenda. They seem to be seeking to remove religion, especially Christianity, out of every phase of public or political life.

In a recent ruling of a California Appellate Court, in *Rubin versus The City of Burbank,* the court ruled that prayers given in council meetings may no longer include the names of specific deities such as Jesus Christ or Allah. It is likely the ACLU was representing Rubin in this case. But what a radical blow to the Christian church. It was obviously directed at the name Jesus Christ. I have given many an invocation at city councils, but I have no knowledge that any invocations were ever given in the name of Allah or any other deity.

In Palm Springs, California the City Clerk sent a letter to all the clergy involved in the rotation of offering prayer before the city council.

In this letter she informed them of this ruling. Some of the clergy objected and pulled out of the rotation.

They call this the separation of church and state, but the Constitution of the United States, including the First Amendment does not say anything about such a separation, as discussed in chapter four.

The local paper came out with an editorial suggesting that the thing to do is to have a different perspective for the "broader good," while omitting the name of Jesus Christ. But to adopt such a posture would be like being an ambassador to a foreign country and having someone tell you that you could no longer let anyone know what country you represent. As the Apostle Paul reminded us in II Corinthians, "We are therefore Christ's ambassadors, as though God were making his appeal through us."[1]

What happened to the second phrase of the First Amendment—"Congress shall make no law...prohibiting the *FREE EXERCISE THEREOF,*" *(capital letters and italics are the author's)* meaning religion in the society? We have gotten so hung up on what we term the "establishment clause," we have almost forgotten the second phrase that gives us true freedom of religion, as our founding fathers intended. The concept of our founding fathers was clearly that they did not want a "state church," and that is what they meant in the phrase "an establishment of religion." They had no idea that some day the phrase would be used to remove Christianity from the daily life of the people.

NOW (National Organization for Women)

This organization has as its stated goal "...to eliminate sexism and end all oppression." It was established on June 30, 1966 in Washington D. C., by 28 original founders. Betty Friedan, author of *"The Feminine Mystique" (1963),* and one of those founders became their first president.

They claim as their current agenda to eliminate discrimination and harassment in the workplace, schools, the justice system, and all other sectors of society, to secure abortion, birth control and reproductive rights for *all* women, end all forms of violence against women, eradicate racism, sexism and homophobia and promote equality and justice in our society.

There methods include marches, rallies, pickets, counter-demonstrations, non-violent civil disobedience, intensive lobbying and class action lawsuits.

They claim to have half a million contributing members and 550 chapters in all 50 states and the District of Columbia.

Economic equality in the workplace—equal pay for equal work for men and women is not an unreasonable goal and is one of NOW's top priorities. Ending racism is another. Again, this is in itself is a worthy objective. But it doesn't stop here. Their strong drive to uphold abortion "rights," their strong posture of gay and lesbian lifestyles and other feminist issues have put them in a camp that is dangerous to the welfare of the family. Their drive to eliminate differences between men and women and their leaving God out of any consideration in their movement put them on the wrong side of most moral and national issues.

We have a very precarious situation here in the United States in regard to women's issues. Back in 1980, President Jimmy

Carter signed an international treaty known as CEDAW, the Convention on the Elimination of All Forms of Discrimination Against Women. Although it sounds harmless, even positive, the language of the treaty while being vague, opens the door to a host of causes that are neither good for the United States or the countries around the world.

Quite recently some of the feminist leaders in the Senate have revived this treaty and have been pushing for its ratification in the Senate. Senator Hillary Clinton is one of players in this latest endeavor.

Attorney Ken Connor, President of Family Research Council, has sounded the alarm, pointing out that if the Senate ratifies CEDAW, United States laws would be changed to redefine the family. He has also noted that the treaty would mandate gender re-education. School curricula would have to be re-written to omit "stereotypes" of women. The idea of "mother" or "mom" is supposed to be outdated. Under CEDAW she becomes "caregiver."

He also noted that the treaty would take away parental rights in favor of the government, a condition which has already been promoted in our country, sometimes successfully.

It would appear that some of the players in NOW are also active in the CEDAW issue. And it is a serious issue, because according to our United States Constitution (Article VI, Section 2) the United States is bound to follow treaties signed by the president and ratified by the Senate. It follows then that ratified treaties supersede state laws and undermine United States sovereignty.

So far I have highlighted only three of the leading organizations that are directing our nation and our world in a very erroneous and dangerous direction. This is not to say that all of their actions are negative. Indeed, some of their platforms and policies could be applauded, but their overall direction is far removed from the direction our founding fathers intended when they formed the great nation of the United States of America.

In addition, of course, there are myriad other players who sympathize with the policies of the above three organizations and play a role in shaping the destiny of America and the world, but

I will not address them at this juncture. Instead I will move on to some of the players who are doing their best to counteract the effects of the above three organizations and any others who would try to divert us away from freedom of religious expression, traditional family values and moral accountability.

CWA (Concerned Women of America)

This organization is probably the largest public policy women's organization with a rich history of twenty some years of service. Their aim is to help their members across the country bring Biblical principles into all levels of public policy. They focus on *six core issues*, which they have determined need Biblical principles most and where they can have the greatest impact. At its root, each of these issues is a battle over world views.

The first of the six core issues is the *Definition of the Family*. CWA believes the traditional family consists of one man and one woman joined in marriage, along with any children they may have. They seek to protect traditional values that support the Biblical design of the family.

The second is the *Sanctity of Human Life*. CWA support the protection of all life from conception until natural death. This includes the consequences resulting from abortion.

The third is *Education*. CWA seeks to reform public education by returning authority to parents.

The fourth is *Pornography*. CWA endeavors to fight all pornography and obscenity.

The fifth is *Religious Liberty*. CWA supports the God-given rights of individuals in the United States and other nations to pray and worship without fear of discrimination or persecution.

The last is *National Sovereignty*. CWA believes that neither the United Nations nor any other international organization should have authority over the United States in any area, including economics, social policy, military and land ownership.

For many of its years this organization was headed by Beverly LaHaye, wife of Dr. Tim LaHaye, well known author, most recently of the "Left Behind" series. Their headquarters are in Washington, D.C. where they have several active departments and a unique blend of policy experts. They have an activist network of people in small towns and big cities across the country, and also work in cooperation with other organizations which share the same values.

TRADITIONAL VALUES COALITION

A classmate of mine, the Rev. Lou Sheldon, graduating from Princeton Theological Seminary in 1960, has headed up a very effective organization to reinforce Biblical concepts and family values. This organization is considered by many in the political scene to be the most effective tool in standing for concerns of Christians in the political arena.

Lou has been the target of brutal and vicious attacks, but has stood courageously in the fight for upholding Christian values and the intent of our founding fathers.

The list goes on with myriad organizations and causes that are seeking to protect and defend America as we once knew it as a moral, God-fearing nation with our greatest asset—freedom. Included in this list would be Dr. James Dobson of Focus on the Family, out of Colorado Springs, Colorado, Dr. James Kennedy with the Coral Ridge Ministries out of Fort Lauderdale, Florida, the American Center for Law and Justice, headed by Jay Alan Sekulow, the Rutherford Institute, the Family Research Council, the Institute for Creation Research, and many, many more.

Of course the ones that are left out and share a tremendous responsibility for the moral decline in our nation and around the world are the movie and television industries, followed closely by the movers and shakers of the Internet.

And then there is the media, that tells us so rapidly what is going on in our world. There has been much debate over the subject, but there can be no doubt that overall there is a liberal bias to the reporting around the globe. The ones who stand for so called "abortion rights" and the supporters of the Gay and Lesbian causes sound loud and frequent, compared to the pro-life and traditional values agenda.

There is no doubt that these battles will be raging in the years to come. Those of us who have lived five, six or more decades recognize all too well the direction our world has gone since the Second World War, but especially since the seventies and Roe versus Wade.

Endnote

1. II Corinthians 5:20 (NIV)

Chapter Eight

THERE IS A WAY

A recent article in our local newspaper related the results of the latest Gallup poll in regard to the strength of faith in the United States. Gallup has been providing an annual index of the nation's religious thoughts and practice for over 60 years. The most recent poll indicates that "an overwhelming 95 percent of Americans continue to profess a belief in God. Nine of 10 freely express their religious preference, and two-thirds hold membership in a church."[1]

What makes these statistics so alarming is that around the globe evolution has been taught with increasing vigor over the last 50 or more years. It's conclusions are that man was not created by God, that man came into existence through a transitional process that took millions of years and that he ascended from lower forms of vertebrates.

It must be that God not only created us in his own image, but that he left his identifying mark in us all in some way and the Apostle Paul understood this and made reference to it when he said, "The requirements of the law are written on their hearts, their consciences also bearing witness..."[2]

But I suppose the news writer, David Yount of the Scripps Howard News Service, who wrote the above article, was also correct when he said, "...there is every indication that religious faith in America, although a mile wide, is only an inch deep."[3]

Now let's take one more look at evolution versus creation:

(1) No logical reasoning of the human mind can come up with the notion that living things have within themselves the ability of self-determination, that is to make themselves into a brilliant yellow daffodil or a giant redwood

59

tree or any other form of life one can imagine. It is totally illogical, no matter how many million years one might add to the transition or the growth process. Since there is design, there must of necessity, by all logical standards be a designer. We will call him Creator.

(2) No research, no fossil records, no new findings have even begun to answer the four problems of the evolutionary theory that Charles Darwin alluded to in his Chapter VI of "Origin of Species."[4]

(3) As a nation and as a world of mankind, we have chosen to hide the knowledge of the Creator and promote a theory that is totally flawed. The apparent reason we have done so is the same problem the Apostle Paul identified, "...what may be known about God is plain to them, because God has made it plain to them. For since the creation of the world God's invisible qualities—his eternal power and divine nature—have been clearly seen, being understood from what has been made, so that men are without excuse."[5]

(4) There is reason to believe that dating methods that are used are based on the rate of material aging today, and are not necessarily proving how material aged in other generations.

(5) Mankind has tenaciously clung to the theory of evolution over recent decades. One of the primary reasons he has done so is that it eliminates the necessity of adhering to moral values and man can therefore be his own "god" and make his own value determinations.

We have chosen to teach a flawed theory as though it were an historical fact of science. The results have been catastrophic throughout our world.

The sexual revolution followed and with it the deterioration of the family along with the lessening of the value of human life. Abortion became the solution, especially for teenagers, to engage in sex without the benefit of marriage and if a pregnancy resulted, abortion was the answer.

America needs a lot more than the overturning of Roe versus Wade, but that would at least be a step in the right direction. Life begins at conception and from that moment you are dealing with a living person. A woman's "choice" begins when she decides to enter into a sexual relationship with a man to whom she is not married. The "termination of a pregnancy" is just another way of saying "taking a human life." No Supreme Court Justice ever had a right to legalize the taking of the life of an unborn child at any stage after conception.

Another facet of the sexual revolution has been the advancement of gay and lesbian causes. At the heart of the issue is the acceptance of the notion that men and women are inherently "that way." The truth is that there is no God given physical anatomy for sexual joining of two of the same sex. All sexual behavior is a matter of choice, whether homosexual or heterosexual. Scripture is very clear that homo-sexuality is a violation of the laws of God and whether you are reading about Sodom and Gomorrah in the book of Genesis, or the laws of Israel that followed, or the teaching of the Apostle Paul in Romans chapter one or any other reference, the truth remains the same—the Bible teaches that homosexuality is outside the will of God. No gay pride parades or political activism in favor of gay and lesbian marriages is going to change the inherent facts.

In my experience of counseling and working with homosexual persons, I have developed respect and love for them because the ones I have encountered honestly think God made them that way. They have also been persons of talent and sensitivity. And it has not been easy when the denomination with which I was connected for 24 years voted in their General Assembly to ordain homosexual persons, by a vote of 60 to 40 percent. The Presbyteries, which are made up of local churches, however, did not ratify their vote.

To summarize my findings on the environment, I am aware what a devastating blow modern industrialization has had on it. I sympathize with efforts to end pollution of highway, forest, sea and air. These efforts are necessary for the preservation of health and the future of our children and grandchildren. However, organizations like Green Peace and others have carried the protection out of reason and beyond law.

Some promoters of the endangered species have also gone far beyond what is necessary and placed the rights of toads and owls ahead of human kind. In a number of cases animal rights groups have done the same thing. Now I happen to be a lover of animals, so much so that I am not willing to hunt a deer or a dove, but I think it necessary to put animal preservation behind the needs and purposes of mankind.

And as for global warming, I believe our president recently made a wise decision when he put off for 10 years any dramatic action in behalf of global warming remedies. You see, as discussed in chapter three, from 1940 to 1970 there was a slight dip in world temperatures to the point where there was some strong concern that the planet would be getting too cold. Since that time there has been a very slight increase in global temperature. Whether the current trend is a natural phenomena or whether it is affected by mankind's activities is not certain. Outstanding scientists have taken both sides.

We struggle in our beloved United States of America over an issue that is really a "non-issue." What is happening is that dominant forces have been parading the "separation of church and state" issue. The truth is that neither the Declaration of Independence, the Preamble to the Constitution, the Constitution itself nor the Bill of Rights say anything about the separation of church and state. That whole idea came in a letter of Thomas Jefferson to the Danbury Baptists fully eleven years after the Bill of Rights was ratified. And even he would be shocked to see and hear what politicians and activists are saying today about the meaning of the phrase. He himself attended Christian services quite regularly in the Capitol building and while superintendent of public schools in Washington D.C. used the Bible and Isaac Watts hymn books as texts.

Our founding fathers clearly meant that they opposed a "state church" such as some of them had experienced in Europe. They did not mean to remove Christianity, the Bible or religion out of public life. In fact, after the so-called "establishment clause," they made sure that Congress was to pass no laws "prohibiting the free exercise thereof." No justices should be appointed to the bench who do not understand our heritage.

Yes, the world we live in is quite different from the one some of us grew up in. We will probably never live to see the day we can relax and not be concerned about enemies within or without, since the new reign of terrorism. September 11, 2001 will go down in history as making that exceedingly plain. But there is a way of preparing for any eventuality.

The wise king stated in a proverb, "There is a way that seems right to a man, but in the end it leads to death."[6] But on the other hand, when Jesus came he said, "I am the way and the truth and the life,"[7] and members of the early church were known as "people of the way."

Yes, there is a way that surely helps put all of the world issues in proper perspective. We live during a time frame that Jesus referred to as "...the year of the Lord's favor."[8] That time frame will come to an end—perhaps in our life time. And the ultimate destiny of this planet is described by the Apostle Peter, "The heavens will disappear with a roar; the elements will be destroyed by fire, and the earth and everything in it will be laid bare."[9] We should be more concerned by these words than we are about the fear of "global warming." We may also take comfort in what Peter wrote further, "...in keeping with his promise we are looking forward to a new heaven and a new earth, the home of righteousness."[10]

It would behoove every reader to take advantage of what Jesus referred to as "...the year of the Lord's favor."[8] What it means is that God is a loving God. In fact we are told by the Apostle John that "God is love."[11] The Apostle Paul lets us know that "In the past God overlooked ...ignorance, but now commands all people everywhere to repent. For he has set a day when he will judge the world with justice by the man he has appointed."[12]

As I am writing we are in that wonderful time when God is seeking to reveal himself to mankind. As a matter of fact one word could correctly describe the Bible. That word is "revelation." God has chosen to reveal himself to us. His love is so unfathomable. He is "...not wanting anyone to perish, but everyone to come to repentance."[13]

God has fully expressed that love by sending his one and only Son into the world. The mission of Jesus was not just to be a great teacher and prophet. In fact, if he is not the Son of God he is not a great teacher or prophet at all, but the biggest deceiver of human history and has perpetrated the greatest fraud mankind has ever known. But if he is the Son of God, then he is the dispenser of God's great love for us. His mission was not only to teach and to preach and prophesy, but to give his life on the cross, as the ultimate expression of God's love The Apostle John said it like this, "This is how God showed his love among us: He sent his one and only Son into the world that we might live through him."[14]

What God asks of us may at first seem like an impossible leap into the unknown, but when we have truly taken that leap of faith, the results are priceless and overwhelming. That "leap of faith" is outlined in the most well known verse of the Bible. "For God so loved the world that he gave his one and only Son, that whoever believes in him shall not perish but have eternal life."[15]

If you are asking, "What does it mean to believe?" the answer is that it is placing your trust for your eternal future into the hands of God's Son, Jesus Christ. When you have truly done that, life takes on a whole new meaning. You become more sensitive to worldly things you once thought nothing about. Your understanding of the Bible begins to open up. In the words of the Apostle Paul to the Corinthian church, "...if anyone is in Christ, he is a new creation: the old has gone, the new has come!"[16]

The same truth is expressed in different ways. In John's gospel it is expressed like this: "...to all who received him (Jesus Christ), to those who believed in his name, he gave the right to become children of God."[17] The Apostle Paul said it this way, "...if you confess with your mouth, 'Jesus is Lord,' and believe in your heart that God raised him from the dead, you will be saved."[18] He went on to say, "Everyone who calls on the name of the Lord will be saved."[19]

I have had people say to me, "I wish I had faith like you do." My answer is this: "You can. It is not a matter of dredging up enough faith to be acceptable to God. It is a matter of the heart, the will. Jesus said on one occasion, "If anyone chooses to do God's will, he will find out whether my teaching comes from God or whether I speak on my own."[20]

Yes, there is a way. It is a way to find inner peace, a new-found joy and a hope that transcends anything offered on this planet. Is it easy? No, it is not, but it is a lot more satisfying than any other offer in this world. Sometimes it means ridicule. Sometimes it means persecution.

To be a follower of "The Way" discipline is required. There are enemies and there is temptation, so reading the "manual" is important.

Getting together with fellow followers is also important. It's called the church. Find one that is truly devoted to Christ and teaches the Bible.

The premises set forth in this book ought not to be brushed aside, but rather emblazoned across the continent and heralded around the globe. Actually the ideas expressed here are embraced by millions, and it is my hope and prayer that you are included among them.

Endnotes

1. *Desert Sun*, Palm Springs, CA, Sat., Jan.18, 2003, page D6.
2. Romans 2:15 (NIV)
3. *Desert Sun*, Palm Springs, CA, Saturday, January 18, page D6.
4. Darwin, Charles, *Origin of Species,* Chicago, Illinois: Great Books of the Western World, Encyclopedia Britannica, Inc.,1952, page 80
5. Romans 1:19-20 (NIV)
6. Proverbs 16:25 (NIV)
7. John 14:6 (NIV)
8. Luke 4:19 (NIV)
9. II Peter 3: 10 (NIV)
10. II Peter 3:13 (NIV)
11. I John 4:8, 16 (NIV)

12. Acts 17:30-31 (NIV)
13. II Peter 3:9 (NIV)
14. I John 4:9 (NIV)
15. John 3:16 (NIV)
16. II Corinthians 5:17 (NIV)
17. John 1:12 (NIV)
18. Romans 10:9 (NIV)
19. Romans 10:13 (NIV)
20. John 7:17 (NIV)

About the author:

Edward George Reitz is currently the Pastor of the Friendship Church, a non-denominational church located in Sun City Palm Desert, Palm Desert, California. For 24 years he was a minister with the Presbyterian Church USA, having graduated from Princeton Theological Seminary in Princeton, New Jersey.

Pastor Reitz also held a California Marriage and Family Therapist license for thirty-eight years, having been trained for two years at the Long Beach Memorial Hospital in Long Beach, California, in Clinical Pastoral Education.

He has had varied experiences including being the first Chaplain at the Hoag Memorial Hospital in Newport Beach, California, Convalescent Hospital Administrator, President and Co-Director of Dove Ranch, a ranch for the homeless in Exeter, California, and Church Pastor.

He is also a veteran of the Second World War, having been a Radio Operator in the United States Navy.

Pastor Reitz makes his home in Sun City Palm Desert, Palm Desert, California with his wife, Jene Sue. They have four children and eight grandchildren.